ANIMAL PSYCHOLOGY FOR BIOLOGISTS

ANIMAL PSYCHOLOGY
FOR BIOLOGISTS

BY

DR. J. A. BIERENS DE HAAN

(LECTURER ON EXPERIMENTAL ZOOLOGY IN THE UNIVERSITY OF AMSTERDAM)

UNIVERSITY OF LONDON PRESS, LTD.

10 & 11 WARWICK LANE, E.C.4

1929

Printed in Great Britain for the UNIVERSITY OF LONDON PRESS, LTD.,
by HAZELL, WATSON AND VINEY, LD., London and Aylesbury.

PREFATORY NOTE

THE contents of this little book consist of a trio of lectures, delivered by the author before the University of London at King's College in early May 1928. The lectures are reproduced here as they were read ; only a few passages that had to be dropped on account of limited time are printed here as they were originally written in the manuscript.

For various reasons it seemed advisable not to change the form in which the matter was offered to the audience : if it had been the intention of the author to write a short introduction to Animal Psychology he would probably have arranged his matter in a somewhat different way from what he did here, where he had to adapt it to the reading of three lectures of limited and equal length.

The author readily seizes this opportunity to thank all those who in any respect helped him to read and publish these lectures ; especially he owes many thanks to the Committee of the Publication Fund of the University of London, who, by a grant from this Fund, greatly aided the publication of these Lectures.

AMSTERDAM,
January 1929.

5

CONTENTS

LECTURE I

LECTURE II

LECTURE III

ANIMAL PSYCHOLOGY FOR BIOLOGISTS

LECTURE I

THE PSYCHOLOGY OF ANIMALS AS AN INDEPENDENT BRANCH OF ZOOLOGY

WHEN I received the honourable invitation of the Academic Council of your University to deliver before you a course of lectures on some branch of Experimental Zoology, I gladly seized this excellent opportunity of coming into closer contact with a country to which I owe so much in scientific matters. For from the time my interest was first aroused in the problems and the work in the field of research which I hope to discuss here before you, it has mostly been English authors or writers in the English language who have given me the best help in stating the problems and interpreting the facts observed. The English-speaking countries have, during the last hundred years, been the places where the interest in the interpretation of animal behaviour has been most animated. When in the second half of the last century Darwin's genius made us realise that man is not a solitary creature, living alone on earth in the midst of an animal world unrelated to him, but that he is the outcome of an evolution that went on for many centuries, and is akin to the animals around him, this insight greatly stimulated the interest also in mental evolution in nature, and consequently in the mental life of animals. And although we are now somewhat sceptical about the value of the methods used in those days, and no more attach so much value to the stories and anecdotes that were collected and quoted to prove the high mental development in animals, and although we are a little more critical too in the interpretation of these stories, yet it would be ungrateful not to acknowledge the significance of the work of men like Darwin, Lubbock and Romanes in the history of our science.

You are of course aware of the fact that about the beginning of this century the methods for obtaining knowledge about the animal mind were much improved, when the well-thought-out experiment in the laboratory or in the animal's natural surroundings was substituted for this collecting of stories of sometimes rather doubtful value. Two names especially must be mentioned in relation to this methodological change, viz. that of your fellow-countryman Prof. Lloyd Morgan, and that of the American Prof. Thorndike. To the latter we owe the introduction of the laboratory experiment in Animal Psychology, a method that suddenly brought the study of Animal Psychology to an unexpectedly flourishing condition, especially in America. But rather than Thorndike, we have to consider Prof. Lloyd Morgan as the founder of modern Animal Psychology, because he first connected careful experiment with critical interpretation, and in his *Animal Behaviour* and *Habit and Instinct* and other works has given us the foundations on which we now build the edifice of our science.

And if finally I may cite two names of men who worked on the theoretical more than on the practical side of our science, I will remind you in the first place of Prof. Hobhouse, whose *Mind in Evolution* certainly is one of the finest analyses of the development of intelligence in animals, and Prof. McDougall, formerly at Oxford, now in America, who in his various works, and especially in his *Outline of Psychology*, made the psychology of animals the basis of the study of the psychology of man.

When I reflect on all this, I rather feel like one who is " carrying coals to Newcastle," speaking on Animal Psychology to people who have in their midst so many first-class authors and workers in this science. If, all the same, I venture to speak here, I have one excuse. I was asked to speak before zoologists, not before psychologists, and, as far as my Continental experience goes, zoologists generally are but slightly acquainted with and interested in this branch of their science. Perhaps matters are different in England, and then my lectures will be rather superfluous. But even in that case, listening to somebody who comes from elsewhere may give you something you did not already know, and the contrast between the new and the old sometimes gives one a new inspiration. So it is only on this assumption that I venture to speak to you.

The subject I wish to introduce to you, i.e. the science of Animal Psychology, forms a borderland between two different sciences, viz. Human Psychology and Zoology, and may be approached from either of these. To the genetic psychologist the psychology of animals provides a body of facts which he may compare with and use for the explanation of those facts that are known to him from the study of the psychology of man, just as for the same purpose he may make useful comparisons between the mental life of normal man and that of the child or primitive man or the criminal. So, in order to deepen his insight in the development of human intelligence, he may study the stages of intelligence in the lower and higher animals, or for a kindred purpose may study the perceptions of animals so far as these differ from or resemble those of man. To give some examples : when we find that some of our sense-illusions are also found in animals, as for instance those concerning geometrical diagrams which Révész demonstrated in hens and those about simultaneous colour-contrast which Kühn could demonstrate even in bees, this proves once more that in man these phenomena cannot be explained as errors of judgment, as was done by Helmholtz in his time. Or when we find in animals some of our human institutions, as for instance monogamous marriage, found even between animals living in herds, we understand that this form of marriage in man is not the outcome of explicit reasoning or moral judgment, but has its roots in the innate tendencies of the species. And now that we are gradually beginning to understand the important part instincts play in the behaviour even of civilised man (and here again the work of Prof. McDougall must be mentioned), the human psychologist will feel the necessity of studying more closely the life of those beings in which those instincts are to be found more openly and less mixed up with the work of education and tradition, and less influenced by conscious reasoning than is the case in man.

Of especial importance for the human psychologist will be the comparison between the behaviour of anthropoid apes and the human child. So Boutan found a correspondence between the actions of the gibbon and the child in the prelingual stage, and Révész compared the faculty of primitive abstraction between children and subanthropoid monkeys. And the brilliant researches of Köhler in the intelligence of the chimpanzee have been a source of inspiration for many recent investigations into the same faculties in children.

But however important Animal Psychology, or, as

in this connection it is generally called, Comparative Psychology, may be for the better understanding of the human mind, the science of the animal mind is more than a mere department of Human Psychology. It is, and will become more and more, a science that is studied *for its own sake*, that is for a better knowledge of the animal, and therefore must be considered as a branch of Zoology. In this respect Animal Psychology has to pass through just such a development as other parts of Zoology had to pass through before it, viz. it has to emancipate itself from the domination of Anthropology, this word being taken in its widest sense. A similar emancipation was reached by Comparative Anatomy when, some fifty years ago, it cut itself off from Human Anatomy, of which till that time it had been regarded as an auxiliary science. A similar battle is fought in these days by Comparative Physiology, which strives to emancipate itself from Human Physiology in order to become an independent science. Needless to say, the reason of this tendency towards emancipation is not a lack of confidence in the capacity of students of Anthropology for doing exact work. The reason is rather that the zoologist feels that the anthropologist cannot be the right man to bring these sciences to all-round prosperity, as with him man will always occupy the central place in his interest, and all his investigations will serve only as means to elucidate the questions that are aroused by the study of man. With the zoologist, on the contrary, no special animal stands in the centre of his interest, all of them have equal rights and equal importance ; so for the building up of really comparative sciences we want the zoologist rather than the anthropologist. And therefore I believe Animal Psychology must be a branch of Zoology rather than an auxiliary science of the Psychology of Man.

The question we zoologists who are interested in all aspects of animal life must ask ourselves is whether there is not in animals something besides the structure of the body, the function of its organs, the phenomena of heredity, variation, growth, and development, something of quite a different nature, related to what we know in ourselves by direct experience as mental phenomena. And if this is so, our next question must be : is it possible to obtain any knowledge about it ? For one thing is certain : if anything of the kind exists in animals, and if it is possible to obtain knowledge concerning it, then all-round zoologists must consider it as part of their task to investigate it, if our science is not to become a mutilated body, lacking a part that may be of great importance. And in this connection it is interesting to recollect that this was already the point of view of Aristotle, the father of Zoology as well as of Psychology, who, to quote Dr. Warden in a recent article, " did not consider his zoological description of an organism or species complete until he had covered its psychological as well as its anatomical, physiological, and developmental aspects."

Let us, then, assume for a moment that such a psychology of animals is possible, and ask ourselves, first, what this part of the science of Zoology will then include. Must we say, as the name of this science seems to show, that it comprises research as to the existence and possible faculties of a *soul* in animals ?

I do not care to define the scope of our science in this way. For the concept of a soul is not one modern Natural Science works with. It has left it to Theology and Metaphysics to discuss the question if there is any principle in us, prior to the body, that will survive its death and destruction. Some centuries ago this problem was also discussed with reference to animals, and the question was asked if we should recognise the souls of our animals, and after death should meet the souls of the same fleas and lice we were worried by during our life on earth. Then came Descartes, who taught that the animal is only a kind of machine and has no soul, and therefore will not survive death, and so settled this question to the satisfaction of everybody.

But if, then, the existence of a soul in animals and the possible faculties of it is not the central problem of this science, what is it we try to investigate when we study the psychology of animals? There are many definitions as to what are the subject and scope of Psychology in general, and it seems to be difficult to find a definition that will satisfy everybody. One of the best, in my opinion, is to define Psychology as the science of *subjective phenomena*, that is, the science that considers as its task the study of those phenomena that are directly related to and experienced by ourselves as subjects.

To illustrate this I can do no better than quote an example from Prof. Stout's *Manual of Psychology*. Let us imagine, he says in slightly different words, a man standing on the seashore and looking and listening to the sea. Then we find in this situation three components, viz. first, the man who stands there looking and listening; then the sea with its rolling waves, producing the sound the man listens to and the movement he is looking at; and finally, the looking and listening themselves, which are activities of the man and processes immediately experienced only by him. So the perceiving of the colours of the sky and of the moisture of the wind are his immediate experiences; but also the recognition of an ocean liner on the horizon, the recollection of former journeys and the desire to leave again for other countries, his feeling of joy or sorrow as he stands there alone in this place. All these are phenomena that are directly related to the solitary wanderer and immediately experienced by him and by him alone.

So Psychology cares for and studies these subjective phenomena, and so, if a psychology of animals is possible, we must define it not as the science of the animal soul, but as *the study of the subjective phenomena in animals*. But with this definition we do not clear away the question of the sceptic : do such subjective phenomena really exist in animals, and if so, will they ever be knowable to us ?

The question whether animals possess a subjective life has not always been answered in the affirmative. I reminded you already of the fact that Descartes declared animals were only complicated machines, without thought or will, although perhaps he was willing to attribute to them some bodily sensations. And although nowadays nobody will believe that his dog or a monkey is no more than a machine, yet kindred ideas have revived in our days in an even more rigorous form, when Loeb, in his Theory of Tropisms, tried to convince us that, at least with the lower animals, actions are only forced movements, governed by external forces as light or temperature or chemical substances, which work directly through the organs of perception on the organs of locomotion, without interference of sensations and effort on the side of the animal. According to this author, the external forces govern the movements of the animal just as the magnet governs the movement of the iron ; there is no real action on the side of the animal, but only passive submission to the working of those forces. Here, therefore, we find a fully anti-psychological point of view, the total negation of a subjective side in the life of animals. In the eyes of men like Loeb and his adherents a real psychology of animals is something impossible.

But there are also other people who, if perhaps not wholly denying the possibility of the existence of something subjective in animals, yet believe that this will never be knowable to us with a sufficient degree of certitude. They therefore consciously ignore the facts of mental life in animals and reject a science of subjective phenomena on methodological grounds, laying stress on an objective way of considering the facts. Therefore they only study the objective reflection of such a subjective life in the outward behaviour of the animals.

Of these " objectivists " the most modern representatives, and probably those best known to you, are the so-called " behaviourists " in America, whose most prominent leader is Watson. Watson denies concepts like perception and emotion and conation, or rather leaves them to the philosopher for further discussion, in the same way as we did with the concept of soul. As material for natural science he recognises only the body of the animal, the stimuli that act upon it, and the reactions of the body on these stimuli or the behaviour of the animal. And he applies this method not only to animals, but also to man. As far as man is concerned, I believe that Watson's position is rather weak, and I cannot believe that he will ever find many partisans to follow his banner. In the case of the animals, however, his system has the fascination of simplicity and of the practical solution of difficulties in its favour. Let us at once acknowledge that Watson with his radical negation of all that is subjective in animals is well within his legal right as long at least as he refrains from calling his science Psychology. For with subjective phenomena his Behaviourism has nothing to do. Only he and his followers make of what might be a blossoming tree of science a leafless stump. The behaviourist always reminds me of the old-fashioned malacologist, who,

2

when finding a living snail, makes haste to kill the animal and throw away its finely built body, and keeps only the lifeless shell as a representative of the whole organism. So does the behaviourist, who, when observing the rich life of the animal in action, deliberately ignores its most essential and important part, and limits his attention to the outer expression of it. The behaviour of animals, as Watson studies it for its own sake, for us is no more than a means to interpret their inner life.

It seems to be worth while asking what may be the psychological reason why in modern times so many voices are heard which, in contrast to general belief, refuse to assume a psychological interpretation of the behaviour of animals. I believe that we may explain this as a reaction against the exaggerations of our fathers, who, especially in the second half of the last century, were rather uncritical when interpreting that behaviour. When in the middle of that century Darwin brought us the belief that man and the animals are united by ties of blood and that the body of man was evolved out of that of the higher animals, there was a tendency, reinforced perhaps by the opposition it had to remove, also to lay stress on the correspondence between the mental life in both. And then, also in consequence of the unsatisfactory method of those days in obtaining material for interpretation, viz. the collecting of stories and anecdotes, communicated by persons of good will but not always able to observe critically enough, there was a tendency to humanise the conduct of even the lower animals and to credit them with the same faculties of intelligence and morals as were found in man. A reaction against this kind of interpretation was bound to come, and it certainly has been the merit of Loeb and others to deliver us from this uncritical anthropomorphism.

But it would be erroneous to believe that there is

no middle way between these two extremes, the somewhat childish Anthropomorphism of the anecdotal school, and the severe objectivism of the behaviourists. A good example of this middle way is found in the attitude of Prof. Lloyd Morgan, whom we may rightly call the father of modern Animal Psychology. His famous canon, formulated in 1895, prescribes that we may not interpret any case of animal behaviour as the outcome of higher mental faculties, as long as it is possible to explain it in terms of simpler ones. This principle was very useful at the time it was formulated, to propagate a more critical attitude. I may observe, in passing, that the canon speaks only of an interpretation in terms of mental processes, but does not require us to explain animal behaviour, as long as we can possibly do so, in terms of objective phenomena, as has sometimes been believed. Yet we must admit that it is only partly true. The danger of such "laws of parsimony" is that they make us forget that it is not the aim of science to explain the facts as simply as possible, but as truly as possible, so that if in those days of exaggerated anthropomorphism it induced a more prudent attitude in the interpreters of animal behaviour, afterwards it involved the danger of causing them to undervalue the complexity of mental phenomena in animals.

So we must not attach too much value to the search for the simplest explanation of animal behaviour, but by careful observations and critical experiments we must rather try to estimate as nearly as possible the quality of the animal's mental activity at a certain moment.

The great difficulty in the interpretation of animal conduct and the study of their mental activity lies in the fact that subjective phenomena are directly recognisable only by the subject who experiences them. We

meet with the same difficulty when we confine ourselves to the study of mental phenomena in our
fellow-men. Here as well we cannot study those
phenomena in other people directly, as we may study
their bodily movements, or, by introspection, study
such phenomena in ourselves. Here, too, we are obliged
to reason by analogy. When we see a man suddenly
crossing a road, having on his face the same expression
as we have when we experience in ourselves amazement
and joy, and when we see him addressing a man on the
other side of the road, we may admit by analogy that
in him the same processes occur as in us when we meet
an old friend, that he also recognises a well-known
face and feels joy at this recognition and tries to go to
that person and speak to him. And this becomes
the more certain to us as we attentively regard him,
observe the change in his face, the sudden stopping
of his walk, and the deliberate change in his direction
and the speaking to the man on the other side of the
road. So we may get some insight into the subjective
experience of our fellow-men by attentively observing
their behaviour.

Surely this is not the only source for obtaining
knowledge of mental phenomena in another man.
For we may talk to him and ask him about his experiences. And he tells us about them in words that
have a special significance and value for us, and so
make it possible for us to judge the nature and complexity of his experiences.

Now, with animals we are in a much more
unfavourable condition as this latter source of information is lacking. No animal can give us a verbal
description of what happens in him, so we shall never
learn anything in this way. Yet the difference is
rather a relative than an absolute one. For even the
man who relates his experiences by talking to us can
only indirectly make us feel what he feels; he can

never make us experience his experience ourselves. And when we talk with peasants or children or natives of primitive races, language becomes a more and more inadequate means of communicating complicated mental phenomena. On the other hand, an animal expresses much of what it experiences through another medium, that may not be so perfect and refined as the language of man, but is often very clearly intelligible to the careful observer. Nobody will misjudge the fear in the attitude and the behaviour of the dog that is threatened with the whip, nor its joy when it is taken out for a walk, although it does not express these emotions in articulate words; neither do we misjudge similar emotions in primitive man, who cannot express himself in our language.

But this interpretation of subjective experiences in other beings by examining their attitudes and behaviour becomes less sure as we descend farther in the scale of animal life and get farther away from ourselves. While the man who knows his animals at every moment sees evidence of mental life in his dogs and monkeys, this changes when we come, say, to fishes or Invertebrates. Attitudes then may be wrongly interpreted, as was the case with ants, who by some authors were described as deliberating together, only because they were found with their heads turned towards each other, or, more naïve yet, with the praying insects, which owe their name to the fact that their anterior legs are bent in a way that reminds one of a praying man. This difficulty in the interpretation of the mental life of lower animals has brought many investigators to the erroneous conception that in these lower orders there is no mental life at all. They forget that the fact that we cannot perceive a thing does not prove that such a thing does not exist. These authors, then, are inclined to draw a line somewhere in the scale of the animal world, and, while granting that above this line psychical phenomena occur, they believe that under this line the assumption of such phenomena is superfluous and therefore obnoxious, and that everything belonging to the behaviour of these lower animals may be explained simply in physiological terms of stimulus and reaction.

But then there arises a new difficulty : where is this line to be drawn ? Let it not be expected that the structure of an animal or of a special organ of it, not even the structure of the nervous system, can help us to find an answer to this question. The structure of an animal, or of its nervous system, can never decide as to the presence or absence of mental life or give us an insight into the complexity of this mental life. No less an authority than Edinger once believed he had a right to conclude that fishes have no memory, from the absence of the neencephalon in them. We now know that fishes do have a memory, and that even much lower animals, as insects or even worms, may be trained to find their way in a simple maze. The nervous system is only the instrument the mind uses to control the body. It will use a simple chain of ganglia here and a complex brain there. But we have never a right to deny mental activity only on the strength of the absence of some particular structure of the nervous system.

This question, then, where to draw a line that separates animals with and without mental life, has been answered in different ways. Edinger drew this line between Fishes and Amphibia, Richet believed that only Vertebrates had consciousness and mental life, Lukas drew the line much lower and believed that only Protozoa and Porifera were devoid of it. But apart from the question where this line has to be drawn, I believe that there is a more fundamental difficulty here. For when in this way we divide the animal kingdom into two halves, one composed of beings that react as machines to external stimuli and are devoid of any perception or feeling or striving, and another composed of individuals that perceive changes in their environment and feel more or less clearly the unpleasantness of bad conditions and the pleasure of better ones and strive to reach a purposed end, then we must ask ourselves how in the course of evolution such a fundamental difference may have arisen, a difference as fundamental as that between animate and inanimate nature.

Some people pass over this difficulty rather lightly by assuming that such mental phenomena may have arisen as a new faculty in the course of evolution as soon as the bodily structure of the organisms reached some special degree of complexity. They compare this, for instance, with the way colour vision was evolved from simply distinguishing between different shades of grey. But the acquirement of the vision of colours is only a refinement of the sense of vision already extant, and does not at all effect so fundamental a change in the nature of the organism as the sudden appearance of mental activity would do in an organism that before was no more than a machine. If we did not believe in the evolution of animal life on earth, there would be no such difficulty here. We could simply admit that one part of the living world had been created as living machines, and the other as perceiving and striving organisms. The gap between the two would no more worry us than the gulf that for the greater part of naturalists exists between animate and inanimate nature. But now that we have accepted the evolution of the higher out of the lower forms of life, we cannot believe that such a fundamental difference between two halves of the realm of living beings can exist. As Wundt has said, a sudden appearance of psyche in the evolution of the animal world would be equivalent to a miracle and is therefore unacceptable to the scientific mind.

Therefore there are, in my opinion, only two consistent standpoints. The one is, that I recognise only my own mental life, directly experienced by myself, as a reality, and regard all other beings, human as well as animal, as complex machines. This strictly solipsistic point of view will probably be accepted by no normal mind. We may, however, extend this recognition to our fellow-men, on account of the likeness of their behaviour to ours, and of what they communicate to us in words. By so doing we shall, with Descartes, separate man with a soul from the brutes without any. It does not seem likely that many evolutionists will share this point of view. But as soon as we grant mental life to other beings than ourselves, we have set the first step on the path that will lead us to the conviction that the only way of escape out of the otherwise inevitable absurdity to our evolutionary thinking is by granting a mental life to all living beings on earth, from man to the amœba, though we may always recognise various degrees of perfection and development. And so mental activity becomes one of the characteristics of animal life in general.

But now perhaps some of you will ask, This sounds all very well, but is it more than a cheap supposition ? Are there any facts that make it probable that some form of mental life, comparable in principle to ours, is existent in the lower animals ? Is there in these lower animals any perception or memory or striving towards an end ?

To answer this question, the best plan is to go to those beings that we believe to be nearest to the root of the tree of animal life, I mean to the Protozoa. Are there any signs of mental life in Protozoa, or is

their behaviour fully explainable in terms of physiological responses to external stimuli ? I am glad I
can appeal to Jennings, one of the greatest authorities
on the life of the lower organisms, in order to answer
the first-mentioned question in the affirmative. In
his classical *Behaviour of the Lower Organisms* Jennings
lays stress on the fact that it is impossible to explain
the behaviour of these animals without admitting
the presence of mental phenomena. I remind you
of his lively description of the Amœba pursuing its
prey with perseverance, trying another way when the
first fails to bring success, making new efforts when the
pursued prey threatens to escape. I refer you to the
instance of experience he found in the Stentor, when
stimulated several times by a stimulus it could not
escape from. I remind you of the great part trial
and error movements play in the behaviour of these
lower animals, and the presence of spontaneous action.
" There is no evidence of the existence of differences
of fundamental character between the behaviour of
Protozoa and that of Metazoa," he writes (p. 263). In
a special chapter he describes a number of subjective
phenomena as occurring in the lowest animals, as
perception, choice, attention, desire, etc. And in
his conclusion Jennings summarises his opinion by
saying (p. 336) : " The writer is thoroughly convinced
after a long study of the behaviour of this organism,
that if Amœba were a large animal, so as to come
within the everyday experience of human beings, its
behaviour would at once call forth the attribution to
it of states of pleasure and pain, of hunger, desire, and
the like, on precisely the same basis as we attribute these
things to the dog."
So here in Protozoa, where probably we find ourselves at the lowest point of the scale of life, we find
undeniable signs of a mental life that in its essence,
although perhaps not in its structure, is comparable

to that of ourselves. So it is certain that the recognition of mental life in these lowest animals is not only a logical necessity of our evolutionary thinking, but is supported by the outcome of a careful study of their behaviour. It would be the more illogical now to deny it in animals that from an evolutionary point of view take up a position between those lowest organisms and ourselves, as insects or worms or molluscs. Not always can it be as clearly demonstrated as with the Amœba. It is especially difficult with sessile animals, which, like plants, probably show a rather sluggish state of mental activity. It was, I believe, Aristotle who first said that plants were animals fallen asleep. Indeed, the sessile life must have a depressing influence on the development of mental activity. The impressions from a life in a monotonous environment with little change must be few, and not much activity is possible where locomotion fails. Animals in such circumstances must easily get into a stage of more or less permanent slumber, and this will not make it easy to show much mental life here. But yet I believe that a close and careful examination of the life of sessile animals will prove to the attentive observer that here too some form of mental life is present. And I may refer again to Jennings, who described it in Hydra and the Sea-anemones.

The last objection I have to deal with is one of a more practical nature. Biologists often ask, What is the use of all this ? Why should we seek for something more, when we are able to describe the behaviour of animals wholly in terms of physiological processes, as reflexes and other simple reactions to stimuli, without the interference of subjective phenomena ? Why should we complicate the description by considering processes that we do not want for our purposes ?

The answer must be, first, that if such a subjective

life really exists in animals, we may not simply disregard it in the description of their behaviour. But apart from this, I believe that it is very doubtful whether such a physiological description will ever cover the whole behaviour of the animals, and that on closer examination of their actions it will become clear that in this way we shall strain the truth and neglect a part of the observable phenomena. There are some examples in the literature of the subject of failures of such physiological explanations. Bethe, at the end of the last century, believed he was able to explain the social intercourse among ants of the same or different nests as simple reflexes to olfactory stimuli, but later observations brought out that there was much more to be found in these actions than Bethe had thought. And some ten years ago Doflein wrote a monograph on the ant-lion, the well-known insect larva, that digs a hole in the ground and waits there for ants and other small insects for its prey, and asserted that the whole behaviour of this animal could be explained by the assumption of three simple reflexes: a " digging-reflex," a " throwing-reflex," and a " snapping-reflex." Later I have controlled this assertion, and in a more careful examination of the living animals I have found that their actions were not at all so simple as to be described as reflexes, but showed a variability and especially a spontaneity that true reflexes miss. This becomes especially clear when we take the animal out of the sand it lives in, and put it in a little box, covered with a glass plate. Then its behaviour is quite different and loses the stereotypy it showed when the animal was in the sand. For instance, it does not close its jaws any more when an ant touches them. Yet there is no mechanical or physiological hindrance for such closing, as is shown by the fact that the animal drove its jaws into the tweezers I touched it with. The new and unusual surroundings exercised an influence on the animal that made it omit the usual reaction of closing the jaws as soon as an ant touched them. This and other simple experiments proved that it is erroneous to believe that everything about the catching of the prey by the ant-lion may be explained by assuming a " snapping-reflex," although in its natural surroundings its actions in their simplicity might give the impression of such a reflex. A reflex would function when the animal was in the box as well as when it was in the sand, and that the catching of the ant is a real action of the ant-lion is proved by the disturbing influence of unusual surroundings. In the same way, newly caged birds will not eat or sing, and caged animals will not mate, till they are accustomed to their new home.

So I am sure that a closer examination of those animals, the behaviour of which is said to be explainable wholly as simple reactions to external stimuli, will bring us more examples in which the proposed physiological interpretation will prove to be insufficient to explain the whole behaviour. Perhaps in the near future it will be part of the task of the animal psychologist to occupy himself more with the lower animals than is mostly done. This work may be less attractive and less grateful than the work on higher animals, where mental life shows such a richness of development, but perhaps it is more important for the moment to discover simple expressions of the primitive mind than to gauge the mental faculties in the higher animals.

But if all this be true, if mental life, be it in a primitive and simple form, is a fundamental character of all living beings, and if, even in lower animals, a physiological interpretation of behaviour fails in regard to the facts observed, then the position of the student of Animal Psychology among his fellow-biologists is wholly changed. Then he need no longer be a humble suitor to the physiologist for permission to incorporate this or that animal into his material, but as a free man in his own domain he declares the whole animal world for his field of research. And putting himself on one line with the morphologist and embryologist and physiologist and other workers in the field of Zoology, he builds up his own science with its own methods and its own ways of explanation, independent of the other branches of Biology.

But before doing so, he has to say a few words to his brother the physiologist, to settle the frontier between their several fields of research. And both agree that if the material they study may from an objective point of view seem the same, viz. the movements of animals, yet their aims are directly opposed to each other. The aim of the physiologist is to analyse these movements into simpler ones, and his ultimate aim is to analyse them into terms of physico-chemical processes. Perhaps he will never reach this goal, perhaps he will even find that it is essentially impossible to reach it, because a factor exists in the living world which is not to be found in inanimate nature and therefore not explainable in terms of physics or chemistry. Be this as it may, the aim of the psychologist lies in another direction. He will not try to analyse the movements of animals into simple material processes, but he will describe them as concomitants or effects of purposeful actions in terms of his own inner experience. He will seek for the perceiving, feeling, striving subject in the moving animal. To give an example : he will not analyse the movements of the lion springing upon the deer into contractions of the muscles of the body, but he will regard these movements as elements of the action of an animal securing its food. Physiology therefore may be said to investigate the movements of parts of the body ; Psychology, on the other hand, investigates the activities of animals as a whole. If both the physiologist and the psychologist agree with this distinction, they may part as friends ; only let the physiologist promise never to give to his science the name " Psychology," as this denotes a tendency of the mind directly opposed to his own. It does not seem very probable that a psychologist will ever call his work " Physiology."

Before finishing I must make one more remark. Perhaps it has struck you that I did not speak about consciousness, and did not ask the question, have animals consciousness ? In former years many attempts were made to find an objective criterion to decide whether at a given moment or in a special situation the activity of animals was accompanied or guided by consciousness. But all endeavours were in vain, and we now know that we shall never have certain knowledge about the consciousness of other beings. Yet I do not believe that this question is so important as used to be believed. Consciousness is a quality of the highest mental processes, but not the essence of psychic life. Modern Psychology has made it clear that in man perceptions and associations and striving may occur without reaching the level of consciousness, and if we were to limit mental life to the phenomena that occur consciously, we should probably disregard an important part of it. So with the animals we do not trouble ourselves very much about this unsolvable question, and study mental phenomena apart from the question whether they are accompanied by consciousness or not.

I am afraid I have been long about it and have perhaps asked too much of your attention. But I believe that for a better mutual understanding it was necessary to expound my point of view first. If in finishing I may be allowed to summarise this point of view in a few conclusions, I would say that Animal Psychology is an *independent branch of Zoology*, independent both from Human Psychology on the one hand and from Physiology on the other. Its aim is the *study of subjective phenomena in animals*, from the highest to the lowest. It may be possible that in some animals that take a low place in the scale of evolution this subjective life is only imperfectly knowable to us for the present. Yet from this fact we do not draw the conclusion that in these animals mental life is non-existent and they are only living machines. In the following lectures then, I hope to give you a short survey of the most important facts the study of this subjective life in animals has afforded us.

LECTURE II

THE ANIMAL AS A KNOWING SUBJECT

In our first lecture we have seen that for the zoologist Animal Psychology is an autonomous, independent department of his science, pursuing its own aims, applying its own methods, and regarding as its own object of study the subjective life of the animals that it studies by observing and interpreting their behaviour. In the two following lectures I will try to give a naturally rather concise review of the principal aspects which this mental life of animals displays. As of course it is impossible to give a full account of the whole matter in so short a time, you will excuse me when I lay rather more stress on those aspects I myself am most interested in.

By introspection into ourselves we know that, although our subjective experiences form one indivisible whole, they show a threefold aspect. Every inner experience has three sides, which, however, are never wholly separable one from the other and can only be isolated theoretically. To use a comparison I read somewhere, they are like three strands woven into a single cord. That is to say, every one of our subjective experiences is partly *knowing*, partly *feeling*, and partly *striving*, or, to use the common technical terms, mental life shows a cognitive, an affective, and a conative side. Our first question now must be, does the same hold good for animals ?

The best way of answering this question is to consider the behaviour of one of those animals that we are best acquainted with, viz. our domestic animals, as the cat or the dog. Let us for a moment call to mind the behaviour of a cat lying in wait for a mouse. Various sense-impressions, as smelling its scent, hearing the sound of its gnawing, or seeing it moving in the corner, give rise in the cat to the perception " a mouse here." This perception is accompanied in her by a feeling of pleasure founded on the agreeable recollections of mice eaten before, and perhaps some feeling of well-being in the anticipation of coming pleasure. But when the mouse does not show itself any more, a feeling of displeasure and per-haps of some disappointment will arise in the cat. Meanwhile the most prominent factor of the mental activity of the cat is its conative side : the concentra-tion of its whole attention on the goal, the effort with all the means Nature gave her to catch the mouse, the careful stealing to the corner, the direction of the eyes and ears to the spot where the mouse was per-ceived, all muscles ready to jump as soon as the prey shall reappear.

I believe nobody who without theoretical bias observes a cat in such a situation will say that I give an exaggerated and too anthropomorphic a descrip-tion and interpretation of what happens with the cat. All the movements of body and limbs are undoubtedly to be understood as expressions of the inner activity of the animal in its triple aspect of perceiving and feeling and striving. Would it not be a lack of courage, then, to say that we shall never know anything about the inner life of our animals, and, with the behaviourists, content ourselves with the objective description of the movements the cat makes, which in this way lose all their inner meaning ?

As I said already, these three aspects of mental life are not distinctly separable. Never does one occur by itself ; the three are always more or less mixed up with each other. But at a given moment one of

3

them may predominate in our experience ; therefore for practical purposes we may regard them as separable here, and speak of the conative, cognitive, and affective life, as if they were independent phenomena. Let us do this here, and let us ask first of all what are the characteristics of animal *cognition*, that is its perceiving, remembering, imagining, thinking, leaving for the next lecture the affective and conative side of its mental life.

The *sensations* of animals have been diligently studied of late years, especially by physiologists. It is chiefly here, where the changes in the outer world touch the mind of the subject, that physiologist and psychologist meet. Yet here too their aims are not quite the same. The sense-physiologist asks, what physical and chemical changes in the external world act as stimuli on the sense-organs and nerves of the animal. The psychologist is ready to accept his results, as this gives him valuable information about the question what the animal senses. The physiologist asks, " Do the vibrations of the air act as stimuli on the auditory organs of the fishes ? Is the eye of the bee differently stimulated by rays of light of different wave-lengths ? " The psychologist asks, " Do fishes hear sounds ? do bees distinguish colours ? " Their methods in this inquiry will be the same, so here physiologist and psychologist may work together as brothers.

The physiologist, however, leaves the psychologist alone when the latter tries to determine the character of the *perceptions* of animals. The important question about the nature of animal perception and its difference from that of man was brought forward some years ago by the work of the German psychologist Volkelt.

Volkelt made some interesting observations about a spider, probably a specimen of the *Zilla* species, which do not wait for their prey in the centre of the web, but lie in wait in a special tube-shaped nest by the side of it. As soon as a gnat flies into the web, the spider comes out of its nest and takes and kills the gnat and drags it into its nest to devour it there. But then Volkelt took a gnat of the same species the spider always had for food and put it, not in the web, but in the tube in which the hungry spider lay in wait. The spider then not only did not attack the gnat, although it presented itself close to the claws of the spider, but even when the gnat approached the spider, the latter took up a defensive attitude against the gnat and finally fled before it out of the tube and into the web.

There is therefore in these two cases a remarkable difference in the behaviour of the spider towards the gnat. When perceived in the web, the gnat is recognised and treated as a harmless prey ; when met within the nest, on the other hand, it is not recognised and regarded as an unknown danger.

Volkelt mentions some other cases of apparent stupidity in animals which show some resemblance to this one. It is a well-known fact that, when a beehive is removed a small distance during the absence of the bees, the returning animals fly straight to the place where the entrance of the hive was before their departure, and accumulate there, unable at once to find the entrance to their home.   It is only after some search that the entrance to the displaced hive is found. And Watson found the same with a tern, which, when its nest was displaced one metre during its absence, flew to the place where the nest was before and had to seek the new place, although its power of vision would certainly enable it to see the nest from a much greater distance.

The explanation Volkelt gives of these facts is the following. It is generally believed, not only among laymen, but even among men of science, that surrounding objects appear to the animals in the same way as they do to us, that is as constant, unchanging images. The dog therefore will see the table and chair of our room, the bird the trees in the field, just as we see them, that is clearly distinguished from other objects in the room and other trees in the wood. Volkelt expresses this by saying that the general opinion is that the animal's world is *dinghaft gegliedert*, split up into separate objects. Volkelt, however, contests this view. He believes that the perceptive image which the animal gets from the world round it is not divided into separate objects, at least not in the first stage. It is only secondarily that special objects may get a separate and predominant place in the complex and dominate the perception. But apart from this, in the animal's consciousness no clear images of separate things arise ; its perceptions are inarticulate and more or less diffuse. The gnat, however important a part it may play in the life of the spider, is not seen by the spider as a separate object, but only forms an element in a greater complex. In the same way the bird does not see its nest as a single object, nor the bee the hive, but these objects are perceived as parts of a greater perception complex, formed by the nest and its surroundings. These complexes then are characterised by their want of separately defined objects, by their want of *structure*, as Volkelt calls it.

These ideas of Volkelt's have been the object of much criticism, especially among zoologists. First of all, his examples do not prove as much as he himself believed. For the case of the bee that cannot find again its displaced hive, Wolf found another and more plausible explanation. Wolf also observed the same confusion of the bees before the displaced hive, but found that this occurs only with bees that are well orientated in the environs of their dwelling. Young

bees that are flying out for the first time, or bees that
are flying out shortly after they are settled in their
new dwelling after swarming, are not disturbed
when the hive is removed a short distance, and fly
directly to the new place. The explanation of the
disturbance in other bees therefore cannot be that
the hive is not perceived as a separate object. The
fact is that, when the bees are well orientated in their
surroundings, they do not find again the hive by means
of vision, but with the aid of their kinæsthetic sense,
the perceptive organs of which seem to be localised
in the antennæ. When the antennæ are cut off,
the bees use their sense of sight again to find the
hive, and then no accumulations arise when the hive
is displaced. The disturbance of the bee therefore
originates in the fact that when returning home by
the aid of its kinæsthetic sense, at the spot where the
hive was before the bee finds itself in an empty place.
With some incapacity to see the hive as a separate
object this has nothing to do. The same is probably
the case with the tern at its displaced nest.

Also Volkelt's other example, namely, that of the
spider fleeing before the gnat, does not prove as much
as Volkelt believed. First of all, it is a well-known
fact that a related species of spiders (*Epeira prompta*)
captures its prey by jumping on it, which certainly
demonstrates that this spider really sees a fly as a
separate object. Further Baltzer showed that it is
possible to feed *Zillas* with living or dead flies
offered to them outside the web, provided that one
of the legs of the spider is touched by the fly. This
proves that, be it by vision or touch, the spider is
quite able to perceive the fly as a separate object,
apart from the web.

Yet I believe it would be wrong wholly to reject
Volkelt's views. I only believe that he went a little
too far when he assumed that no single objects are

perceived by the animals. I believe it is very probable
that in general the perceptions of the animals are of a
more complex and less detailed character than our
own. It has been observed by several investigators
that in general the animal does not so much react to
single objects as to a whole situation. This was
already Thorndike's opinion and expressed by him in
several places of his *Animal Intelligence*. " A certain
situation brings forth a certain act," he says in this
work, " the whole situation sets loose the impulse."
And so Volkelt can frequently appeal to the authority
of Thorndike in support of his views.

I myself on two occasions found instances that
brought me to a similar opinion, viz. that in the
perception of the animals single objects, even objects
that by their own nature or by training are of vital
importance to them, do not come so much to the
fore as would be the case with us. I believe with
Volkelt that animals in general react to a whole
situation, and often show a curious incapacity out of
such a complex to isolate fragments that must be of
great importance to them and are unable to recognise
these fragments in other complexes. One of these
cases I found when studying the instinctive reactions
of the common cuttle-fish, *Octopus vulgaris*. As you
are undoubtedly aware, this animal feeds principally
on crabs, which are discovered and caught when they
are swimming or creeping on the ground, and it is an
interesting fact for the naturalist to observe the
clearness of vision of the octopus in discovering the
faintest movements of the crab on the ground, its
signs of attention and emotion when the crab is
discovered, and the ability and strength with which
even a big lobster is caught and mastered. Now
everyone would probably suppose that such an important object as is the crab to the hungry octopus will
be recognised in every situation. But this is not

the case. When in Naples I offered to a hungry octopus a crab that was not swimming freely in the water or creeping on the floor of the aquarium, but was hanging in the water before him, fastened to a thread, the octopus, although it gave signs of observing the hanging and vehemently moving object in the water, made no effort to catch the crab. When I raised the crab, so that it hung above the head of the octopus, or when I let it sink, so that it hung only a few inches above the floor, this did not change the attitude of the octopus. But as soon as I let the crab sink down to the floor and gave it an opportunity to crawl round there, while attached to the thread, then at once the octopus, with a vehement colouring of the whole body, jumped on the crab and had enveloped it with its suckers before I could rescue it by drawing the string.

And even more curious was the result on another day, when to obviate the criticism that perhaps the crab had hung at too great a distance from the octopus, so that some short-sightedness of the octopus might have played a part, I slowly moved the string with the sprawling crab towards the octopus, which was sitting quietly in a corner of the aquarium. When the crab was only a few inches away from the eye of the octopus, this animal, apparently troubled by the object hanging so close to it, directed its sipho on the crab and tried to blow it away by pushing out a stream of water. This stream of water gave the crab a swinging movement, and after some moments the swinging crab with one of its legs touched the body of the octopus. This was too much for the cuttlefish, and again a violent spout of water was directed towards the harmless crab to push it away. The crab, however, remained sprawling and tried to find a support on the body of the octopus. Then came a moment when by accident the crab touched one of the suckers of the octopus, and this movement was fatal to it : in no more than a fraction of a second the octopus wrapped its arms around the crab and brought it to its mouth !

This observation proves that a hungry octopus, ready to jump at any crab that appears before its eyes, does not recognise the crab in the unknown situation of hanging in the water, although the object itself is very well perceived. (That at the end the crab was recognised by the chemical sense, localised especially in the suckers of the octopus—a sense that forms no special images of the objects like the sense of vision does—is another thing, and has nothing to do with the question that occupies us here.) This not recognising the crab is just as curious as would be the case of a man who was in the habit of feeding on apples, but who should recognise this fruit only when lying before him on the table, not when hanging on the tree. It proves that the perception that in octopus gives rise to the instinctive actions of jumping and seizing the prey is of a complex character, namely, that of the crab making the special movements of swimming or creeping. Another complex, that of the crab sprawling on a string, does not give rise to the usual reaction. This shows, too, that the octopus is unable to detach the principal object from the new situation and to recognise in it the same object that was the centre of the other more usual situation.

Experiments with other octopus gave similar results. Always there was either no attacking of the crab as long as it was hanging in the water and seizing it as soon as it was crawling on the floor, or at least a great uncertainty towards the hanging object. Vehement coloration proved that the crab was always observed as a new object in the neighbourhood, but with the exception of one animal I never saw direct attack on the hanging crab. Once, for instance, I saw an octopus cautiously approaching a hanging crab, looking at it carefully for some moments, and then moving slowly and cautiously the tip of one arm to test the suspicious object. Here, too, there was no recognition of the crab in the unusual position. It was not the object, but, to quote Thorndike again, the whole situation, that set loose the reaction.

Other instances of animals reacting to a whole situation and not to a single object out of it I found when training a young Pig-tailed Macaque (*Nemestrinus nemestrinus*). When, for instance, this animal was trained in a choice-apparatus with five swinging doors to seek a piece of fruit behind a door over which was a card with a special diagram, it suddenly got somewhat confused and made errors when it found all five doors unlocked, instead of finding only the positive door unlocked, as had been the case during the training. I myself could scarcely discover in front of the apparatus which doors were locked at the back, and that the monkey saw it certainly proved a keen power of observation. But that it was somewhat confused when the doors were suddenly found unlocked, proved that the animal was not trained to go to the special card, but to the complex: " that diagram over the only unlocked door of the apparatus." Therefore, when suddenly all doors were unlocked, so much was changed in the situation as to make him confused for some moments. I will add at once that a few moments afterwards the monkey got back its certainty of choice, even when all doors were unlocked, so that it would be wrong to suppose that it had been trained not to choose the special diagram, but the only unlocked door. Nevertheless this confusion proved that it was not trained with regard to a single object, but to a complex.

Even more clearly I found this in other experiments with the same animal. In a choice-apparatus with

two doors I had trained it to find its food behind the
door that was marked by a card with a red circle, while
over the other door a card with a blue triangle was
placed. When the animal was well trained, I changed
the blue triangle for a blue circle or a red triangle,
leaving the red circle as it was. Had it been trained to
go simply to the red circle, as I supposed it was, then
there would have been no reason for the monkey to
make errors now, as the red circle remained visible
as before. Instead of this, the animal now made
about 50 per cent. errors—that is, it was quite confused. The only possible explanation of this sudden
confusion, as all other circumstances remained the
same, is that again the animal was not trained simply
to go to the red circle, but to go to the red circle in
opposition to the blue triangle, so that, when this
latter figure was changed, the red circle lost its
meaning as a guide to the food. As soon as I showed
the former combination of figures, the animal was
again at home and made no more errors.

I could adduce other instances of the same and
another monkey that show that they are not trained
to go to single figures, but to figures in a special complex. I rather prefer to mention some instance of
similar confusions in other animals. Buytendyk and
Hage trained a dog to go to the middle one out of
eleven doors in a multiple choice-apparatus. When
the dog was sufficiently trained, the apparatus was
turned round 180°. The room had windows on both
sides, so the illumination of the apparatus and the
doors was not changed. Yet the dog was wholly
disorientated now, and could only find the right door
after seeking for it for a long time. The explanation
must be that the dog was not trained with regard
to one single characteristic, as, e.g., the direction
it had to choose when entering the apparatus, but was
orientated to a complex of characteristics of various

kinds, kinæsthetic and visual ones, the latter from inside and outside the apparatus. As the apparatus was turned round, this complex was disturbed, and the dog had to learn anew how to find its way to the right door. Similar results were found by Buytendyk when working with toads.

I need scarcely mention that all this cannot be explained physiologically by the qualities of the structure or functions of the sense-organs of the animal. The monkey, for instance, is quite able to see and distinguish an isolated red circle, and a blue triangle too. The fact that it reacts, not to the isolated figure, but to the complex of figures and apparatus therefore is not to be explained by the organs of vision functioning in a special way. But it would be equally wrong to seek for an explanation of these facts in some peculiarity of the intelligence of the animal and say, for instance, that in the new combination the monkey no longer understands that the same is asked from him as before. It would be wrong, I believe, to assume that an animal in training is explicitly aware of a problem that is placed before it. It seems more in accordance with the facts to believe that during the training some more or less complex image gradually acquires the meaning of an indicator to the reward. And when, in the way described above, we disturb this complex image, it loses its meaning for the animal, and as a consequence of this disturbance, the training object is no longer recognised as such in the perception of the animal.

All this now is in agreement with the conceptions of modern human psychology. In former times it was generally assumed that sensations were the stones with which our perceptions were built up. Nowadays it is mostly assumed that in the beginning our perceptive experiences form complexes without clearly defined boundaries or relief, and that only during the course of mental development they become articulate and divided into minor parts, and so gradually we become able to distinguish even single small details of the complex. In the animal, now, this splitting up of the original complex seems to go less far than with man, therefore the perceptions that give rise to its reactions have in a higher degree the character of complexes, of "situations," than with us. Yet the difference between the two is only relative and not of an absolute nature.

But it is time to finish our speculations about the nature of animal perception, and to pass on to other sides of animal cognition. Here too we shall find differences with man, and we shall find that the whole of the cognitive life of the animals takes place on a more primitive level than with us. This, for instance, is the case with *memory* and *imagination*. There seems to be no reason to assume that an animal ever sits down and calls to mind the events of the past day. The caged tiger does not show evidence of carrying in its memory the days when it walked freely in the jungle, nor the dog at home the walk it took some hours before. The animal lives in the present, is bound in by the impressions of the moment. Of course this does not mean that the animal has no memory ; the capacity of profiting by the experiences of life shows that the faculty of retaining impressions is widely spread, even among lower animals. But the memory of the animal has a more dependent character than ours and is bound up with sense-experiences. When by training or the experience of life a special object or situation obtains a special meaning for the animal, as, e.g., the boy that always throws stones gets a special meaning for the dog in the street, or the red circle in the apparatus gets a special meaning for the monkey in the laboratory, the renewed perception of those objects awakes anew the feeling of something " alarm-ing " or " promising " in the mind of the animal. Yet the animal never shows any evidence of remembering or anticipating these feelings when it receives no sense-impressions that in some way or other are connected with their reappearance. And also there is no reason to believe that at the moment the animal reacts in the same way as before to a special situation, it realises that the situation of the moment is the same as the one it reacted to in a special way some time ago. The acquired meaning of the situation colours this situation in a special way, and this causes a reaction that comes naturally to the animal, just as it is a natural thing for it to drink water when it is thirsty.

And no more than in the past does the animal live in the future. It need scarcely be said that the bird building its nest or the digging wasp burrowing its hole do not perform this work aware of some necessity in the future. However purposeful these actions may be, they are caused by special sensations or perceptions, probably mostly of bodily origin. Köhler made some observa-tions of his chimpanzees about their reckoning with the future. He only found indications of it when this future formed a part of an intended action of the animal itself, for instance when the animal, in order to reach a fruit that it could not seize with its hands or get by the use of a single stick, made a sharp point to one stick to put it in another, and so procured itself a longer stick. Yet such an action was observed only when a fruit that was out of reach was in sight ; never did he see a chimpanzee make such a double stick when there was no immediate need for it. The animal lives in the present, and in a present of rather short duration.

Another question, related to but not identical with this, is the following : have animals *free ideas*, independent of perceptions, independent therefore of what is directly presented to the senses ?

You are perhaps aware of the fact that Thorndike, after careful experiments with dogs, cats, and monkeys, answered this question in the negative. I need not give a description of these experiments, that have become classic as the first well-thought-out laboratory experiments in our science. Hungry animals were brought into various kinds of cages which they could open by a simple action, as the raising of a lever or the pulling of a cord, and food was laid before them outside the cage. The animals now had to learn to open the cage in order to obtain the food, and, according to Thorndike, learned this gradually by selecting out of the several random movements they made those that were useful to their purpose. So they learned to obtain the food by a process of trial and error, not by the aid of systematic thought or a clear idea of what was to be done.

That they did not form ideas of the necessary movements seemed the more clear as they were not able to learn to open a box by seeing it done before their eyes, whether by the experimenter or a fellow-animal. They did not even learn to do it by being put through the action, that is, they did not learn the trick when the experimenter took the legs of the animal in his hands and in this way performed the necessary movements. The learning of the animals, according to Thorndike, is therefore comparable to that of a man who is learning to skate on the ice or to ride a bicycle. This man too has no clear ideas of the movements he must make, but special perceptions of a mainly kinæsthetic nature get connected during the process of learning with some special reaction and afterwards are always followed by it. So the animal does not learn to open a box by forming an idea of the movements it made the day before or might do now, but only by linking special movements to special sense-impressions. It is not even necessary that these movements should be logically connected with this result : Thorndike trained a cat to lick or scratch herself when she wanted the door of the cage to be opened. On the other hand, it was proved that it was necessary to have these movements done through an impulse of the animal itself, as movements done passively and without any impulse of the animal itself, as is the case when animals are put through certain movements, were not associated with the success obtained.

Other investigators, perhaps somewhat influenced by the authority of Thorndike came to similar results with other animals. But in later years some opposition arose against the conclusive force of Thorndike's experiments. First of all, it appeared that it was not so certain as Thorndike had believed that animals cannot learn by imitation. Several instances were adduced of animals that were unable to find the solution of a problem alone, but did the right thing after having seen another animal perform the act. So Haggerty and Kinnaman found clear instances of imitation in monkeys, and Berry found the same with cats and rats, Porter with birds, and Katz with hens. In all these cases the animals first observed the act of a fellow-animal and then afterwards did the same themselves, although before they had not been able to find the way to do it. It cannot be denied that in such cases some idea of the act, done by its fellow, must have guided the animal in its action. Here certainly some idea of a system of action must be intercalated between the perception of the situation and the reaction of the animal to it.

But Thorndike was equally wrong in assuming that animals cannot learn by passive movements, by being put through the action. Here the experience of the trainers of animals in circuses speaks against him, as many of the tricks animals have to perform are taught by performing the movement with the animal. But also some instances of the effect of this passive training are known from the laboratory. So Cole found instances of such a way of learning with raccoons. Some of his animals that during some time had repeatedly been placed into a problem box and rewarded when they had succeeded in opening it, afterwards went into the box spontaneously by their own means. So they showed that they had associated the being placed into the box with the obtaining of the food and now made themselves the movements which before they had been passively put through. And Cole succeeded in teaching four animals the opening of a box by this method of putting the animal through the trick, even when the animal by itself had not been able to find the solution by trial and error. In all these cases it was clear that the animal was guided by ideas of what it had done before when put through the action by the experimenter.

But there are also indications of a more general character of the existence of free ideas in the animal mind. Animals often clearly seek special objects that cannot be perceived by their senses. Cole's raccoons sought their milk-bottle, and the loop the cage was to be opened with. Dogs often seek invisible objects, for instance, the ball they are accustomed to play with. Köhler's chimpanzees sought food that had been buried the day before, and when in such cases seeing the place again where the fruit had been hidden may have revived the image of the hidden fruit, yet an idea of the invisible fruit must have existed in their minds.

Now, it is a curious fact that some of these images of things not present to the senses seem to be innate. Such must be the case with animals that build complicated nests, without being guided by examples they can imitate or a tradition they can follow. Here I do not so much think of the web-building of the spider, which is a relatively simple work, determined by the natural movements of the animal and the dimensions of its limbs, as of some elaborate buildings of birds and mammals, like the beaver. And when in the latter perhaps some imitation may play a part, this cannot be the case with the bird that only in the first days of its life sees the nest it is bred in, and then afterwards builds its own nest according to the scheme common to the species. Here no tradition or imitation can play a part, and as the building is too elaborate to be described as a simple piling up of the necessary material, we must admit that the bird builds its nest after an innate idea of it, while being driven by an internal impulse which we call the instinct of construction.

In all such cases we have indications of the existence of free ideas, free from what is directly present to the senses. Perhaps this seems to you to contradict our previous statement that animals do not call to mind past experiences. I grant that if such free ideas of absent objects are present in its mind, the animal might sit down and recall the past. But there is no reason to believe that the animal ever does. In all the cases mentioned before, the ideas of absent things were always called up by other sense-impressions that in some way or other were related to them. Even the image of the nest is only called up in the bird in a special period of its sexual cycle and probably emerges only after bodily sensations of a special kind. Present sense-impressions are the only stimulators to action in the animal; the animal is bound in by the impressions of the moment.

But what when sense-impressions from the outer world are excluded, when in sleep the animal is

4

detached from the outer world ? May it be that then images of experiences of the past are evoked in him ? In other words, may we assume that animals are able to *dream*, and experience in their dreams images just as we do ?

More than two thousand years ago Aristotle, that keen observer of animal life, believed that animals dream as we do, and the layman who observes his dog barking in its sleep and moving its legs as if it wants to run away generally holds the same opinion. But often other opinions are heard. That higher animals, especially dogs, make movements in their sleep that may be interpreted as expressions of vivid dream-images, no one will deny. But the question is, is there any reasonable ground to do so, or must we admit that these movements are caused by some bodily sensations, vaguely perceived during their sleep? The latter opinion was held by Thorndike, for instance, who denied the existence of dreams in animals, as he did not admit the existence of free ideas. On the other hand, some investigators credit animals with vivid imaginations, and the capacity of dreaming, like Romanes, who even believed that crocodiles dream. Some twenty-five years ago now the Italian psychologist Sante de Sanctis collected observations of animal dreams among those people who had the best opportunities of observing animals in their sleep, viz. breeders and hunters. That most of them believed that dogs dream is not so astonishing ; more important was the general statement that the movements we observe in sleeping dogs are generally correlated with the experiences the dog has had during the past day. Especially when that day had given some strong excitement, as hunting or fighting with other dogs or sexual intercourse, the animals in their sleep often made movements that might be interpreted as expressions of reminiscences of such experiences. So it is made very probable that at least the higher animals dream in a similar way as we do, and then resuscitate in their mind images of former experiences.

In this case, therefore, we may say that animals in some way have the capacity of resuscitating the past without the aid of new sense-impressions. But as I said before, such a revival probably occurs only then, when impressions from outside are prohibited by sleep. The animal is the slave of the present moment, and it is probably only in its dreams that there is a short and rare emancipation from the impressions of the environment, a faint anticipation of that mental activity that raises man so greatly above the animal.

But then, if the animal has free ideas as distinguished from direct sense-impressions, what is the nature of these ideas ? Are animals able to form abstract ideas, abstract concepts? do they combine and order them? do they draw conclusions from these combinations? do they *think*? The answer must be that there is no reason to believe that animals ever form abstract concepts and draw conclusions or reason. In this matter we must tread cautiously and remember Lloyd Morgan's prudent rule, not to explain by higher mental faculties what may with equal probability be explained by lower. To give one example I found in Holmes's *Animal Intelligence* : Romanes once told a story of two dogs, the larger of which had a bone that the smaller one wished to get. As soon as the larger one left the bone for some moments, the smaller one tried to take it, but then the larger one defended its possession and drove his friend away. Now, after some time the larger dog went out of the room without being noticed by the other. A few moments later the larger dog barked in the garden ; then suddenly the smaller dog went straight to the place where the bone lay and took it. Now, Romanes believed that there was here a case of reasoning on the side of the smaller dog ;

" My friend is barking out of doors, so he is not in the room, so I may safely take the bone." It is clear, however, that an explanation on a lower level of intelligence is also possible and even more probable. After some bad experiences, the smaller dog was prevented from trying to get the bone by the mere presence of the larger one. The hearing of the larger dog barking at a distance now removed in the smaller dog that feeling of constraint that in the presence of the larger dog had hindered him from doing what he had liked to do, and gave him back a feeling of freedom. The first thing he did then was to go and take the bone. It is clear that there is some element of intelligence in the action of the small dog, but not such explicit reasoning as was supposed by Romanes.

Other apparent instances of reasoning in animals are found in those cases where animals act as if they try to deceive us. Such cases are readily interpreted by less critical observers as signs of reasoning in their pets. Yet I believe these too occur at a much lower level of intelligence. To a dog that from experience knows that his master does not allow him to do something he would like to do, that thing acquires the quality of something dangerous, especially when his master is present. When the master is not present, this quality may disappear, and the act may be done. But when at that moment the master reappears, the act just done gets again its quality of something dangerous, and the dog tries as soon as possible to change his activity to other things, if possible far away from his master. Hempelmann tells a case of a dog that was forbidden to come near the dung-heap in a corner of the garden. When his master called him when he was there, the dog did not go straight to his master, but first went behind some bushes in another corner of the garden, and only from there went straight to his master. To the uncritical mind this may seem a proof of slyness in the behaviour of the dog, but an explanation is possible on a lower level of intelligence: dung-heap and master were two dangerous objects for him, and his first impulse therefore was to fly away from both, till in the other corner of the garden he lost this feeling of fear, and then answered the call of his master.

It will be clear that here, too, there is no reason for assuming any genuine reasoning on the side of the dog, a combination and comparison of concepts and a drawing of conclusions. Other instances of alleged reasoning will also find a more probable explanation on a lower level of intelligence. The faculty of forming abstract concepts and of working with them is limited to man, but still we find, especially in the higher animals, a kind of practical intelligence, an understanding of the relations of things and an insight into the results of their actions which is sufficient for the needs of practical life. In my last lecture, I hope to speak about the animal as a feeling and striving subject, and at the same time I hope to say some words of this practical intelligence in higher animals.

LECTURE III

THE ANIMAL AS A FEELING AND STRIVING SUBJECT

In our second lecture we have seen that the mental life of animals, like that of ourselves, may be divided, if more or less artificially, into three activities, that of knowing, of feeling, and of striving. We saw that none of these activities ever occurs quite alone, but that they always follow each other and are linked together, although at a given moment one of them may dominate the other. And in the same way as in our second lecture we considered the animal as far as it is a knowing subject, we shall now have to consider the two other sides of its subjective life, viz. that of its *feeling* and *striving*, that of affection and conation.

I need scarcely warn you that there is some danger of ambiguity in the word " feeling," as in common speech it is used in different senses. So it may be used to indicate the sense-experience of touch or temperature, for instance when I say that some object feels hard or cold, or some internal bodily sensations, as when I say I feel hungry. Feelings of this kind of course belong to the cognitive side of mental life. The same is the case when I say I feel that this or that is true, that is, when I know that it is true, without being able to prove it explicitly to myself or others. By the term " feeling " the psychologist only understands the experience of something as being pleasant or unpleasant, and in a more complicated form those experiences we name " emotions " and " sentiments."

The affective life of animals has the peculiarity that, while it lies rather open to us in the higher animals as monkeys and dogs, it is almost as a sealed book to us in the lower animals. The affective life of the higher animals has so much in common with that of ourselves and the expressions of it are so much like our own that it is relatively easy to understand it, and certainly easier than to understand what the animal at a certain moment observes or remembers. We can feel with our dog his joy in a walk, his anger when meeting the neighbour dog, his disappointment when we do not allow him to go out with us. All this we understand directly when observing the expression of his feelings by the attitudes and movements of his body and the sounds he utters. Nobody who knows his animal well will be deceived here.

But the case is far more difficult with animals like the insects or worms that show no resemblance to ourselves in their movements and expressions. When we disturb a nest of ants and see the inhabitants running about at a greater speed than before, rushing to and fro without any perceivable goal, we may safely draw the conclusion that some strong emotion has broken out and that the action of the animals is caused by some common feeling of anger or fright. And when we see a worker bee that has found a new store of food coming back to the hive, dancing about, and see how she is soon followed by a number of other bees, so that a general commotion is caused in the hive, we may safely infer that the return of the animal bringing with it the tidings of a new store of food has aroused some common feeling of joy or expectation. But in general the body of the lower animals, so differently built from ours, does not give us much information about the feelings its owner experiences, and their movements are generally unintelligible to us as far as they express affections.

On the other hand, it would again be erroneous to believe that the fact that we do not understand them may be regarded as an argument for denying the existence of any affections in lower animals. Perhaps *a priori* some of you will be somewhat sceptical about the existence of the feeling of fear in the crab and believe that nothing of the kind will ever be demonstrable. Yet Piéron and Roskam found that crabs that were hung in an aquarium on a string, fastened to one of their legs, did not autotomise the leg, even when they were slightly teased by the experimenter. But as soon as an octopus was brought in the neighbourhood of the crabs, they at once threw off the leg and fled. The same was found in some insects that autotomised a leg when they were held up before a mantis. I believe I am not very bold in assuming that this sudden vehement reaction before an enemy is provoked by a strong emotion of fear or fright.

Therefore, as our standpoint has been that mental life is a characteristic of all animals, we must admit, by analogy of what we know directly in ourselves and observe in the higher animals, that the lower animals too have their feelings of pleasure and displeasure, their fears and frights, though possibly these feelings and emotions are of a lower intensity and occur in a dimmer state of consciousness.

Now, it is a fact of great biological importance, that the feelings and emotions of one animal are generally felt and understood sympathetically by other animals of the same species. This mutual understanding is brought about by the same means that we understand our animals by, viz. by their attitudes and sounds, so by what is called their bodily and vocal language. But this language shows one characteristic difference with the language of man. While our language generally is meant to communicate something, that of the animals is no more than an expression of their own feelings and emotions. But these expressions are understood by other animals of the same species, and so secondarily get the meaning of a means of communication. I believe this difference between human and animal language holds good even in the case of the mother animal giving a warning cry when some danger threatens her young. Spectators are then often inclined to believe that the mother uttered the cry with the explicit intention of warning her young. I do not believe that this is true. For the danger is felt as threatening herself as well as her offspring, or, better perhaps, herself in her offspring, and so her cry is in the first instance only an expression of fear, but is secondarily understood by the young as announcing some danger, so that they quickly seek a place to hide themselves. And in the same way when one animal in the herd feels a strong emotion of anger or fear and expresses this by a particular attitude or sound, the other animals understand it, and by a function Professor McDougall has called the "*sympathetic induction of emotion*" the same emotion arises in them too and causes the whole herd to act together, whether in attack or in common flight.[1]

---

[1] It will be clear that I am here only referring to the natural language of the animals. In the more intelligent of our domestic animals, however, we sometimes find cases of an endeavour to communicate special desires or wishes, of which the "begging" of our dogs is the best-known example. In these cases special attitudes or sounds of the animal have got linked for him, through habit or training, with special rewards, and the animal now intelligently knows how to use these attitudes to obtain the result desired. There seems to be no reason for assuming that such an acquired language, which approaches to a certain degree the true language of man, is also used by the animals in their natural intercourse with animals of the same or other species.

Now, it is an interesting fact that these utterances of emotions are often understood, not only by members of the same species, but also by animals of other species. We know that herds of zebra and ostrich often keep together, and when the sharp-sighted ostriches discover some danger and show signs of alarm or fear, the zebras understand these signs and are so enabled to fly in time. When in the Alps chamois and marmots are frightened by some danger, such as the approach of man, both utter their fright by a peculiar whistle. Although the sounds of either are different from the other, yet by experience they learn the meaning of each other's sound and fly as well at each other's whistle as at that of an animal of their own species.

These two cases were taken from animals that in wild nature live together in the same surroundings. It is interesting to see how animals that are brought together from different places, and never meet in their natural state, yet sometimes understand each other from the first moment. So Furness tells us that the chimpanzee understands the danger-cry of the orang, although he himself never makes the same sound. But there are also many instances of a curious misunderstanding of each other's language in animals that are brought together from different places, for instance in the cages of the zoological gardens. So baboons as a sign of friendly approach make a special sound, caused by a repeated smacking of the lips while the mouth is very slightly opened. The mandrill, on the contrary, when expressing the same sentiment, raises the corners of its mouth and shows the canines. The result of this different expression of the same sentiment is frequently a quarrel when these monkeys are first brought together, as the showing of the canines means a menace of fight in the language of the baboon. Fortunately, after some time the animals learn to understand each other's attitudes.[1]

It is of course impossible to give here a full account of the whole affective life of animals. I only wish to draw your attention to one particular part of it that has been put in a new light by some recent investigations, namely, that of the *sentiments of relative rank* that appear to exist among animals living together in a herd, in other words, the sentiments of subordination and domination. These sentiments have especially been studied by the Norwegian biologist Schjelderup-Ebbe, in the first place with the domestic hen. We know that when animals with social tendencies are brought together, whether by the chance of life or under the influence of man, soon an association is found among them and they are bound together by a network of social relations. One of these is the arrangement of the members of the herd into different ranks. Between two of these animals it is soon settled which is the master and which is the subject, and in the poultry-run this is recognisable by the fact that the master may peck at the subject, who lacks the courage to peck back, and can only save himself by retreat. The result of it is that in the poultry-house there exists, according to Schjelderup-Ebbe, a fixed social precedence, in which one animal, No. 1, may peck at all others, No. 2 may peck at all the others with the exception of No. 1, and so forth, till at the bottom of the list we find one miserable animal that is pecked at by all the others, and finds no one to peck at itself. This order is not based on brute force alone ; the animal that at the first meeting shows fear or uncertainty towards the other will probably become the subject. This gives the explanation of other more complicated relations : as many factors, mental as

[1] I owe these particulars to Mr. A. F. J. Portielje, Inspector of the Amsterdam Zoological Gardens.

well as corporal, decide which will be the master, it may be that, for instance, hen No. 1 subjected hen No. 2 by greater force, No. 2 subjected No. 3 by greater courage or impetuosity in a fight, while No. 3 frightened and impressed No. 1 at a moment that the latter was in bad health or by some other reason was in an unfavourable mental condition. The subject revolts but seldom against the master, and then a new battle is the result, in which the future relation between master and subject is settled. Such revolts generally arise, then, when the subject notices that the master is in a bad condition.

When new hens are introduced into an already existing society, their chances of getting a good place and precedence are small. The other animals that are already familiar with the place and feel stronger by the fact of belonging to the society show a much greater self-confidence than the newcomers, who are somewhat depressed by the unknown surroundings and their inhabitants. The same holds good for other animals that are introduced into a new group, for cows, for instance, that are brought into a new meadow with other cows, for monkeys brought into a new cage in the Zoological Gardens. And those among us, who feel somewhat less confident in strange surroundings than they feel at home, experience sentiments that in their essence are related to those of these animals in similar conditions.

A curious case of such precedence in a small society I observed myself when working with monkeys. I had brought together in a cage two young monkeys, a male Mangabey (*Cercocebus fuliginosus*) and a young Pig-tailed Macaque (*Nemestrinus nemestrinus*). The mangabey was the taller and stronger of the two and evidently dominated his fellow, who at that time was not in very good health. As I never saw them fighting together, I suppose that this precedence came about in the same way as with the hens, namely, simply by a threat from the stronger animal. The macaque was so afraid of the mangabey that when the latter only looked at his mate, and especially when he raised his eyebrows so that his white eyelids became visible, the macaque threw down the food he had in his hand and fled into a smaller cage in a corner of the living-cage. But now, when I threatened the mangabey by gestures or looks, he did not offer resistance to me, feeling himself inferior to me ; but, on the other hand, wanting to assert himself, he turned towards the other monkey and from a distance looked at him in such a way that the frightened animal fled into the smaller cage. So sure I was of this behaviour that when I had to isolate the smaller monkey in the cage before going to work with the larger one, I only had to threaten the latter with my fist ; then he looked at the smaller one, who directly fled into the small cage.

But once when I wished to show this proceeding to the keeper, who every day brought food to the animals and cleaned the cage, the result was quite different. Now when I threatened the mangabey with words or gestures, he did not turn against the other monkey but against me, and began to attack me and to scream at me. The same happened when I kept quiet but the keeper began to threaten him. Then again he attacked me, instead of defending himself against the keeper. The reason was that when I was alone with the monkeys, I was No. 1 of this small society and was respected as such by both. But the keeper, who entered the cage every day to clean it, had become an even more important person than I was. So when I threatened the monkey in the presence of the keeper, the animal took courage from the fact that this higher authority was near him and remained neutral. And again, when this higher authority threatened him, he now felt so much the superiority of the keeper over me that he dared attack me as one of lower rank.   And when the keeper went away it was curious to see that, when the monkey and I were threatening and screaming at each other, the monkey at once changed his attitude, gave no more the slightest sign of resistance, but looked for the smaller monkey to vent his rage upon.

Again a different situation was formed once when I wished to show this to a visitor whom the monkey had not seen before.   When I threatened him then, he did not attack me nor look at his mate, but began to attack the unknown visitor, who, as he had never let the animal feel his superiority, seemed to be considered as an inferior being.   And again it was interesting to see that when I began a sham fight, either with the visitor or with the keeper, the monkey took a part in this fight from the inside of his cage by screaming and jumping at us, and then always took the part of the higher in rank, that is to say, my part when I fought with the visitor, and that of the keeper when I fought with him.   His social instinct made him feel a danger when the head of the herd was attacked and induced him to assist him, and it was certainly surprising and somewhat disappointing to see how this feeling of the rank of the different persons predominated over sentiments of personal affection.

I have told you this to show how in so simple an animal community as the poultry-farm or the monkey-cage there may come into being a rather complicated system of social relations, based on the sentiments of superiority and inferiority, and how even human beings are regarded as having a place in this graded organisation.   Chance has here lifted a tip of the veil that generally covers for us the affective life of the animals.   Would it be too bold to suppose that if it was possible for us to cast a glance at the other sides of their affective life, we should there also find more complicated sentiments than are often supposed to be there ?

But it is time to pass on to the last aspect of mental life, viz. its conative side, and consider the animal as far as it is a *striving* subject. Again I must repeat that it is somewhat artificial to look upon the striving of animals as if it were something apart, unconnected with other mental experiences. On the contrary, striving is always ushered in by sensations or perceptions, whether internal or external ones, and itself provokes feelings of pleasure and displeasure, which in their turn may influence the direction the effort takes. The significance of internal bodily sensations, such as hunger or sexual stimulation, as springs of activity has been studied of late by different physiologists, especially in America ; let us therefore here limit ourselves to such striving as is provoked by external stimuli, and first regard those that are caused by simple physical or chemical stimuli, such as light or gravitation or temperature.

The reactions of animals to such simple sensations has been the field of research of the much-discussed Theory of Tropisms of Jacques Loeb. I will not discuss this theory in detail, the less so as at the moment it has chiefly but an historical value. I will only remind you of the two principal features of it, viz. first, the assertion that the movements of an animal to or from a centre of stimulus are caused by some direct action of the stimulus on the organs of perception and through them on the organs of locomotion, in consequence of which the animal turns round till its body is symmetrically stimulated and an equilibrium of both sides of the body is obtained ; and then the second assertion, that all this happens mechanically by physico-chemical changes in the perceptors and effectors, without any real activity on the side of the animal, so that this theory implies a negation of any real effort in the animal.

This mechanical theory of animal movement, however, as I told you already, has not been able to stand the criticism of later years and has had to stand aside for the more modern theory of animal taxis. By the term *taxis* we understand a movement of freely moving animals with regard to simple external stimuli, as a ray of light or gravitation. Kühn divided these movements into four classes, one of *tropotaxis*, in which the animal directs itself symmetrically with regard to the stimulus, movements that correspond fairly well with the tropisms of Loeb, and then one of what he called *menotaxis*, that is, movements in which the animal keeps a fixed direction with regard to the stimulus, so for instance keeps in a fixed angle with the direction of the light. As examples of these movements I refer you to the so-called " compass movements " of ants and other insects, as they are described by Santschi, von Buddenbrock, and others. Kühn's two other classes comprise movements that are to be estimated as higher, and do not concern us so much for the moment. So under *mnemotaxis* he understands movements in which memory plays a part, as in the return of the animal to its nest or hive, and under *telotaxis* movements that are directed towards a simple object as a goal. For these last two higher classes of movement the term " taxis " seems to be somewhat out of place.

Now, it has been shown by the researches of the last few years that these tropotactic movements, which outwardly show resemblance to the tropisms of Loeb, form only a small part of the directed activity of animals. Yes, it has even been asked if such tropotactic movements really occur at all, or if they had not better be explained as movements directed to a goal, as telotactic movements, to use Kühn's terminology. I believe, however, that recently some observers have been able to describe movements of lower animals that show the characteristics of a tropotaxis, viz. an endeavour to change the direction of the body, till it is symmetrically stimulated by the stimulus or stimuli that act in the field, and to move forward while retaining this symmetrical stimulation. But this must not be supposed to mean a resurrection of Loeb's theory, that this adjustment takes place passively by a direct working of the stimulus on the sensory and locomotion organs of the animal. We must understand all these tactic movements as innate reactions to simple sensations, as for instance the distribution of the light in the field, reactions that generally have biological value to the individual or the species, are variable in their issue and may be changed by the experience of life.

It is scarcely necessary to mention some examples of this biological meaning of the tactic movements of animals. The positive reaction of the caterpillar of Porthesia brings it to places where the best food in the form of young leaves is to be found, and when after feeding the reaction to light is inverted, new movements bring it to a place from where, when again hungry, it may attain other places where food is to be found. Animals that are indifferent to light or gravitation may suddenly direct their movements to or away from it in case of danger. So the flies that fly round in our rooms without showing orientation to the direction of the light, as soon as they are chased become positively phototactic and fly to the window. Young tadpoles when brought together in a tank will swim without orientation to light, but when a greater number of them were brought together in a small vessel, Franz found that they suddenly become clearly positive to the direction of the light. Deterioration of the *milieu* may have the same effect, so Daphnias get

5

positively phototactic when brought into water with dioxide of carbon. Other water-animals become negatively phototactic in case of danger and fly to the bottom of the water to escape from their enemies. For the theory of tropisms such sudden changes in the sign of the reaction are inexplicable, especially when they arise as results of the suddenly appearing danger. They are only intelligible when we regard them as innate reactions to simple sensations, comparable in essence to the more complicated reactions we shall soon have to consider. And in the same way it becomes intelligible that the experience of life or the training by the experimenter may induce the animals to change these innate reactions. So Szymanski and Turner succeeded in training cockroaches to avoid the dark corners of an apparatus by applying electric shocks as soon as they entered them. Blees gradually trained positively phototactic Daphnias to move away from the light. Such changes of tactic movements by training must be inexplicable to those for whom these movements are a direct effect of the stimulus on the locomotory organs, as was assumed in Loeb's theory.

Also a closer inspection of the way tactic movements are performed shows us that they generally do not occur in such a mechanical way as was assumed by Loeb. The movements of the animal towards the light are generally not so straight as that of the iron towards the magnet. There is much of trial and search in them. They are therefore described by Jennings and others under the name of " *Trial and error movements*," or " *Searching movements*." This type of reaction to stimuli takes up an important place among the reactions of animals, lower as well as higher, and forms a typical characteristic of animal conation, in contrast to the mechanical reactions of inanimate nature.

But returning to these tactic movements in general, it is clear therefore that we must consider them as innate reactions to special simple sensations. In other cases, and especially with higher animals, the innate reactions are not so simple, nor are the perceptions by which they are evoked. Still, it is only a difference of degree that distinguishes them from the reactions we considered just now. These more complicated innate reactions are generally known as *instincts* or, better, as instinctive actions, and as long as mankind has studied nature this instinctive life of the higher animals has always been a source of wonder and admiration.

I do not believe it is necessary for me to mention instances of these instinctive actions, the most remarkable of which we find among the insects. Fabre in his brilliant *Souvenirs entomologiques* has given us a number of such cases which fill us with admiration of the wonders of animal behaviour. And certainly the most wonderful feature of them is the seeming intelligence in the actions of the animal, a seeming insight into what is necessary for the moment and the means to reach that result. When we see the solitary wasp, before laying its eggs, digging a hole somewhere in the ground, and then going out in search of one special animal, as a spider or some insect, and as soon as it is discovered paralysing it by stinging it on or near one of the ganglia and dragging it to the hole as the suitable food for the unborn larva, nobody is at first able to forgo the impression that the wasp acts on the understanding that it is necessary to feed the creature that will come out of the egg, and shows insight into the means to attain this end by storing a stock of fresh food for the larva. Yet we know that there is here no real understanding and that the actions of the wasp are done in an almost automatic way, comparable more or less to the way a child recites a poem it has learnt by heart, but the contents of which are beyond its understanding. So with the wasp, too, the meaning of its actions is beyond its understanding, and therefore these actions often show a remarkable lack of adaptation to small changes introduced into the conditions by the experimenter.

Fabre, who always laid stress on this automatical character of instinctive actions, has given us many instances of this lack of adaptation. Though it may be that he was somewhat biased by theoretical conceptions, it is no less true that the animal, while performing one of its complicated instinctive actions, is devoid of all insight into the meaning of its own doing. And as no other creature taught the animal to do what it does, we must assume that it brought with it into life a special structure of the mind, by which certain perceptions are always followed by certain more or less complicated actions.

That the instinctive actions, that the conative side of this system of cognitions and conations linked together, may be of a very complicated nature I need not repeat again. I only wished to remind you of a fact I told you in our last lecture, to show that the perception too that gives rise to such actions may be of a more complex nature than is often realised. I mean the case of the octopus, that did not jump at the crab when it was in an unknown position, but only when it was perceived crawling or swimming. This complex of the instinctive actions of going towards the crab and jumping at it from a proper distance and bringing it to the mouth with the suckers is therefore not evoked by the relatively simple perception of a crab, but only by the perception of a crab moving in a special way. In a similar way Volkelt's spider acted only on the complex perception of the gnat moving in the web. So I believe that just as we find degrees of complication in the actions of animals, from the simple moving in the direction of the light of a phototactic animal to the complicated system of actions that is for instance performed by the queen ant, when after returning from her nuptial flight she has to procure a living for her future offspring, so in the same way we may find degrees of complication in the cognitive side of the instinctive process, from a simple sensation of light in Daphnia to the so much more complex perceptions of the higher animals.

But in all these reactions the most essential part is the innate mental structure the animal brings with it into life, *a priori* of all experience, which links together perceptions and actions to a unity of biological significance. We are especially indebted to McDougall for drawing attention to this mental structure as the core of the problem of the instincts, in contrast to many other authors, who generally gave definitions of this concept, in which only the effective side, the instinctive actions, were regarded.

Now, this concept of instinct has passed through a long history, and even at present we cannot say that there is a general agreement about its significance and its value for Animal Psychology. Originally it was meant to denote the spring of all the actions of animals, while, on the other hand, all actions of man were attributed to reason. We do not make this distinction now ; we know that in animal action, too, there are other elements besides the instinctive ones, and that, on the other hand, there is much that is instinctive in the actions of man. Some authors, however, totally reject the concept of instinct, saying that it is an obscure and unanalysable one that only serves to cover our ignorance of the real motives and causes of animal action. I do not see the necessity of rejecting a concept only because it has not been further analysed. The aim of natural science is to explain the facts nature offers us, and one of the methods towards explanation is ranging them under general concepts of wider scope. The concept of instinct at present serves this purpose very well and may therefore be used, even if it should afterwards be replaced by something else that will better account for the facts. So physicists used the concept of ether to explain different phenomena in nature, until other theories made this concept superfluous. So also at present the concept of instinct is a useful one to unite different facts of animal behaviour. Our task for the moment is to enlarge our knowledge about these innate modes of action in the animals and to seek for general rules that govern them.

But, while there is no reason to ban the concept of instinct as being obscure, we must confess to great ignorance as to the question, how in the course of the evolution of animal life the various modes of instinctive actions, often differing in remarkable details from one species to another, may have developed out of each other, or found their origin in other modes of activity. As long as man believed that all species were created at the beginning, and had remained unchanged since that moment, there was of course no difficulty, as the mental structure was as typical of the species as its anatomical or physiological characteristics. But now that we believe that the present animals have developed out of more primitive ancestors, we must ask ourselves how this mental structure may have developed too. So far no satisfactory explanation seems to have been offered. According to the Lamarckians, instincts developed out of the habits of the ancestors, so that the instincts of the offspring are genetically fixed modes of action of former generations. But apart from the difficulty that this presupposes the heredity of individually acquired characters, a heredity that, as you know, has so far found but little support among biologists, there is the more difficult question, what was the nature of these actions of the ancestors ? We cannot believe that they were intelligent actions, that, for instance, the ancestors of the wasps really understood the necessity of storing food for their unknown off-spring. And of course it is incredible that they should have imitated other beings or were instructed by them. But, on the other hand, the theory that instincts may have originated in a selection of small accidental varieties in the actions, of which those that were advantageous to the species were kept and transmitted to the offspring, while the obnoxious ones disappeared (as was assumed by Weismann and others), is no longer acceptable. For it will always remain unexplainable how by accidental variations the complicated and yet so marvellously harmonious actions of some insects may have been built up. The origin and development of instincts seems to me to be one of the greatest puzzles of our evolutionary belief and one of the most difficult to solve.

While, then, we do not understand how instincts may have developed, on the other hand, we do know that they may change, at least during the life of the individual. The innate instincts of young animals may be moulded and changed by the experiences during their natural life or by the experiences they gather in the laboratory by the will of the experimenter. This possibility of the moulding of instinct by ex-perience proves, of course, that instincts are not so rigid and devoid of all plasticity as has sometimes been believed. The higher we come among animals, the greater is this plasticity, and the more therefore instincts lose their character of special reactions to special perceptions and only keep the character of general tendencies of reaction. So, for instance, the specialised instinct of the parasitic wasp which seeks one special species of spider or locust as food for its future offspring is enlarged in the higher beasts of prey to a general tendency to hunt all larger moving animals.

This change of the instinct by experience, as McDougall has already pointed out, may take place in the perceptive as well as in the effective part of the whole complex of perception and reaction. So by experience the perception that evokes the instinctive reaction may become more specialised than it was at first. Lloyd Morgan's chickens, for instance, first reacted by pecking at all small objects they perceived, as pebbles, their own toes, etc., but gradually learnt to distinguish between what was edible and what not, and limited the pecking reaction to such objects as in their experience had obtained the meaning of good food for them.   In like manner the animal may learn to react to new objects in the same way as it did before to others. So animals in a country where man is rare at first may show confidence in him, which, however, changes into fear as soon as they have experienced that he is as dangerous as other beings they are afraid of. And on the other hand, the reaction to special perceptions may be changed by experience, as in the case I mentioned before of the cockroach which avoided the dark corners of the apparatus after being punished there by an electric shock, or when an animal that never showed any preference for a special colour has learnt by training to go to that colour in order to obtain a reward.

This study of the moulding of instinct by experience is certainly one of the most fascinating parts of animal psychology. We know that we need not go to the higher animals to find instances of it ; even an animal as low in the scale of animal life as the earthworm may be trained to go to the right or to the left in a T-shaped tube, by rewarding the choice of one side and punishing the choice of the other, as has been shown by Yerkes and others. This means that while at first, when seeking a hiding-place in the apparatus, the perception of the bifurcation of the tube does not evoke any special reaction, the experience of feeling an electric shock after turning to the left and finding a reward in the form of a dark place when turning to the right causes the perception of this same bifurcation to be at last always followed by a turning to the right. I need not tell you how complicated a system of alleys can be learnt in this way by the higher animals ; the different kinds of mazes have become important laboratory instruments for measuring the capacity of animals for forming motory habits under different conditions. And in the same way problem boxes have become important instruments for measuring the capacities of different animals for moving special latches and bolts that at first had no meaning for them in order to get at some visible but otherwise unattainable food.

While in all such cases the original reaction therefore is gradually changed by acquired experience, the actions of higher animals may sometimes be guided by other functions of the mind than innate modes of activity and influenced by other factors than gradually working experience. In the higher animals a sudden change in the issue of an action may occur, suddenly an old way of proceeding may be abandoned or suddenly a new one may be adopted. This sudden change is then the result of a higher mental process than the profiting by experience was, and is based upon an *insight into the relations of surrounding things*, an implicit understanding of the connection of causes and effects, of the results of their own actions and of the movements to be made to obtain a certain result. As I have said before, it would not be right to call this process " thinking," although it is certainly related to it and may be regarded as a primitive form of our conceptual thought. For there is no reason to believe that in the animal there is explicit formation and combination of ideas of what will be the effect of certain actions, an explicit choosing of one out of many possible ways of proceeding. Hobhouse in his elaborate analysis of the growth of animal intelligence has called this function " *practical judgment.*"

In this type of action, animal striving reaches its highest form. With the help of this insight into the relation of things the animal may carry out adequate actions in situations it has never been in before, that is without being guided by an innate mode of behaviour and without being taught by experience gained before. This guidance by practical judgment, however, does not wholly exclude all influence of previously gained experience ; only the experience in this case is of a more general description and would by itself not be sufficient to help the animal in that particular situation. The experience in this case differs, for instance, from that which is gained by repeatedly running through a maze ; every time the centre of the maze is reached the animal has acquired a special experience that will enable it to run through the same maze with fewer errors the next time, but will not give it any help when another time it is placed in a maze of a quite different construction. In the case of practical judgment, however, the animal may have acquired a general experience about the properties of things that may serve for a basis to this practical judgment. So the monkey that has learned to open a problem box by drawing a bolt and lifting a latch will generally do the same as soon as another box is given to him that is closed by another combination of bolts and latches, and will so show that it has a general understanding about the meaning and working of bolts and latches. A dog, however, in similar circumstances will generally not be able to do so much, and, when placed in a new problem box, will not be able to apply the experience acquired in the old one, but will have to learn the opening of the new box anew by making different useless and useful movements.

This function of practical judgment in its more elaborate form is probably limited to the Vertebrates. I once sought it in an Evertebrate animal that generally stands in an odour of intelligence, viz. the octopus. The problem I placed before it was very simple. I placed an obstacle between it and a visible prey, so that it only had to take a short and simple roundabout way to get it. But the animal could not solve this problem, although in its life it had had plenty of opportunities to gather experience about the effect of turning round stones and rocks, and obstinately continued trying to reach the food in a direct way. No trace of such practical judgment, therefore, was to be found here. But, on the other hand, this function is not limited to the higher Vertebrates alone. McDougall and Helson found striking instances of it in the white rat, an animal that is often believed to be good only for running through the different mazes human fancy can devise. Squirrels, too, are described as hauling in ropes in order to obtain food that has been hung on them. And the faculty of making simple roundabout ways to a goal that cannot be reached in a direct way may be observed in many animals, for instance, in hens, although it often requires much time and much ineffectual running to and fro before suddenly the way to reach the goal is seen by them.

For all that, the highest and most interesting forms of this practical judgment are to be found in the highest mammals, and especially in those cases where they prove to be able to use, or even to construct, *tools*, that is, to use and construct objects not belonging to their own body as means to reach an otherwise unattainable goal. Recent work of Köhler and

Yerkes with Primates has given us many instances of such a use of sticks or ropes to draw in fruits that lay out of reach of animals, dragging boxes to a place where fruit was hung too high to be reached by hand, and even of animals that piled up two or more of such boxes in order to build a platform that might serve them to reach the goal.

This free use of tools is to be found only, or nearly only, with anthropoid apes. But in lower animals, especially in the lower monkeys, we find something we may regard as an elementary form of this faculty, and that I would call " *the faculty of intelligently utilising the possibilities of the movements of things.*" So lower monkeys, for instance, very soon understand how to move a turning table, when a piece of fruit is laid on it out of their reach, and directly turn it round with their hands, till the fruit may be seized. In the same way they draw in a rake, when in front of it and out of their reach a piece of fruit is laid. But when in such a case the fruit is laid not before but beside the rake, then they are generally unable to lay the rake behind the fruit and draw it in, as an ape would have done. And up to now no monkey or lower animal has proved to be able to construct its own tool, as did the chimpanzees of Köhler, that broke branches off a tree in order to obtain a kind of rake with which to draw fruit into their cage. In this respect we find again a gradation among the animals that approaches to but does not reach the level of man, who alone is able in the mind to design tools of a far more complicated structure and to realise them in matter, tools suited to purposes far away in time or space, and greatly exceeding the wants of the moment.

I must finish now, not for want of material, but because the time has expired. I hope I have been able to give you the impression that for the biologist too, Animal Psychology is a field of study, rich in problems, and full of promise. It is a very satisfactory fact that in the last decades this part of Zoology has found a renewed interest in different countries. If I should have awakened in some of you some interest in a till now unknown field of research, or, even better, the desire to work in this branch of science yourselves, then my visit to your University will give me a double satisfaction.

REFERENCES

LECTURE I

A. Bethe : " Dürfen wir den Ameisen und Bienen psychische Qualitäten zuschreiben ? ", *Arch. ges. Physiol.*, 70, 1898.

J. A. Bierens de Haan : " Reflex und Instinkt bei dem Ameisenlöwen," *Biol. Zentralbl.*, 44, 1925.

L. Boutan : " Le Pseudo-langage : Observations effectuées sur un Anthropoïde : le Gibbon (Hylobates leucogenys Ogilby)," *Actes Soc. Linn. Bordeaux*, 67, 1913.

F. Doflein : *Der Ameisenlöwe*, Jena, 1916.

L. Edinger : " Have Fishes Memory ? ", *Ann. Rep. Smithson. Inst.*, 1899.

L. Edinger und E. Claparède : *Ueber Tierpsychologie*, Leipzig, 1909.

L. T. Hobhouse : *Mind in Evolution*, 2nd Ed., London, 1915.

H. S. Jennings : *Behaviour of the Lower Organisms*, New York, 1906.

W. Köhler : *The Mentality of Apes*, New York, 1925.

A. Kühn : " Ueber den Farbensinn der Bienen," *Zeitschr. für vergl. Physiol.*, 5, 1927.

J. Loeb : *Forced Movements, Tropisms, and Animal Conduct*, Philadelphia, 1918.

F. Lukas : *Psychologie der niedersten Tiere*, Wien, 1905.

W. McDougall : *Psychology, the Study of Behaviour*, London, 1912.

W. McDougall : *An Introduction to Social Psychology*, 18th Ed., London, 1923.

W. McDougall : *An Outline of Psychology*, London, 1923.

C. Lloyd Morgan : *Animal Behaviour*, 2nd Ed., London, 1920.

C. Lloyd Morgan : *Habit and Instinct*, London, 1906.

G. Révész : " Experiments on Animal Space-perception," *Brit. Journ. Psychol.*, 14, 1924.

G. Révész : " Experimental Study in Abstraction in Monkeys," *Journ. of Comp. Psychol.*, 5, 1925.

G. F. Stout : *A Manual of Psychology*, 2nd Ed., London, 1921.

E. L. Thorndike : *Animal Intelligence*, New York, 1911.

C. J. Warden : "The Historical Development of Comparative Psychology," *Psychol. Rev.*, 34, 1927.
J. B. Watson : *Behaviourism*, New York, 1924.
W. Wundt : *Vorlesungen über die Menschen- und Tierseele*,
6e Auflage, Leipzig, 1919.

LECTURE II

F. Baltzer : "Beiträge zur Sinnesphysiologie und Psychologie
der Webespinnen," *Mitt. Naturf. Ges. Bern*, 1923.
C. S. Berry : "An Experimental Study of Imitation in Cats,"
Journ. comp. Neur. Psych., 18, 1908.
C. S. Berry : "The Imitative Tendency of White Rats,"
Journ. comp. Neur. Psych., 16, 1906.
J. A. Bierens de Haan : "Versuche über den Farbensinn und
das psychische Leben von Octopus vulgaris," *Zeitschr. für
vergl. Physiol.*, 4, 1926.
J. A. Bierens de Haan : "Ueber Wahrnehmungskomplexe
und Wahrnehmungselemente bei einem niederen Affen,"
Zool. Jahrb. Abt. allg. Zool. Physiol., 42, 1925.
J. A. Bierens de Haan : "Der relative Wert von Form- und
Farbenmerkmalen in der Wahrnehmung des Affen," *Biol.
Zentralbl.*, 45, 1925.
F. J. J. Buytendyk et J. Hage : "Sur la Valeur de Réaction de
quelques Excitants Sensoriels simples dans la Formation
d'une Habitude par les Chiens," *Arch. Neerl. Physiol.*, 8,
1923.
L. W. Cole : "Concerning the Intelligence of the Raccoons,"
Journ. comp. Neur. Psych., 17, 1907.
M. E. Haggerty : "Imitation in Monkeys," *Journ. comp.
Neur. Psych.*, 19, 1909.
F. Hempelmann : *Tierpsychologie vom Standpunkte des Bio-
logen*, Leipzig, 1926.
S. M. Holmes, *The Evolution of Animal Intelligence*, New
York, 1911.
D. Katz und A. Toll : "Die Messung von Charakter- und
Begabungsunterschieden bei Tieren (Versuche mit Hüh-
nern)," *Zeitschr. für Psychol.*, 93, 1913.
A. J. Kinnaman : "Mental Life of Two *Macacus rhesus*
Monkeys in Captivity," *Amer. Journ. Psychol.*, 18,
1902.

W. Köhler : "Zur Psychologie des Schimpansen," *Psychol. Forschung*, 1, 1922.

J. P. Porter : "Intelligence and Imitation in Birds," *Amer. Journ. Psychol.*, 21, 1910.

Sante de Sanctis : *Die Träume*, Halle, 1901.

H. Volkelt : *Ueber die Vorstellungen der Tiere*, Leipzig, 1914.

E. Wolf : "Ueber das Heimkehrvermögen der Bienen," *Zeitschr. für vergl. Physiol.*, 3, 1926.

LECTURE III

G. H. J. Blees : "Phototropisme et Expérience chez la Daphnie," *Arch. Neerl. Physiol.*, 3, 1919.

W. H. Furness : "Observations on the Mentality of Chimpanzees and Orang-utans," *Proc. Amer. Philos. Soc.*, 55, 1916.

H. Helson : "Insight in the White Rat," *Journ. Exp. Psychol.*, 10, 1927.

A. Kühn : *Die Orientierung der Tiere im Raum*, Jena, 1919.

W. M'Dougall and K. M'Dougall : "Notes on Instinct and Intelligence in Rats and Cats," *Journ. Comp. Psychol.*, 7, 1927.

H. Piéron : "Recherches sur l'Autotomie. De l'Existence d'une Autotomie psychique superposée à l'Autotomie Réflexe," *Arch. int. Physiol.*, 5, 1907.

J. Roskam : "Quelques Observations sur la Nature de l'Autotomie chez le Crabe," *Arch. int. Physiol.*, 12, 1912.

Th. Schjelderup-Ebbe : "Beiträge zur Sozialpsychologie der Vögel," *Zeitschr. für Psychol.*, 88, 1922.

Th. Schjelderup-Ebbe : "Zur Sozialpsychologie der Vögel," *Zeitschr. für Psychol.*, 95, 1924.

J. S. Szymanski : "Modification of the Innate Behaviour of Cockroaches," *Journ. of Anim. Beh.*, 2, 1912.

C. H. Turner : "An Experimental Investigation of an Apparent Reversal of the Light-responses of the Roach," *Biol. Bull.*, 23, 1912.

R. M. Yerkes : "The Intelligence of Earthworms," *Journ. of Anim. Beh.*, 2, 1912.

R. M. Yerkes : "The Mental Life of Monkeys and Apes, A Study of Ideational Behaviour," *Beh. Monogr.*, 3, 1916.

R. M. Yerkes : "The Mind of a Gorilla," *Genet. Psychol. Mon.*, 2, 1927.